the little book of
ANCIENT CHINESE THERAPIES

Published by OH!
20 Mortimer Street
London W1T 3JW

Text © 2020 OH!
Design © 2020 OH!

Disclaimer:

ISBN 978-1-91161-084-7

Editorial consultant: Sasha Fenton
Editorial: Victoria Godden
Project manager: Russell Porter
Design: Ben Ruocco
Production: Rachel Burgess

A CIP catalogue record for this book is available from the British Library

Printed in Dubai

10 9 8 7 6 5 4 3 2 1

the little book of
ANCIENT CHINESE THERAPIES

angela mogridge

CONTENTS

INTRODUCTION

Traditional Chinese Medicine (TCM) is an ancient system of health and wellness that has been practised in China for 5,000 years. In the West, TCM is considered a form of complementary or alternative medicine; however, it is still very much part of China's modern healthcare system. Whereas "mainstream" medicine treats the illness, TCM treats the whole body, so it provides a more holistic approach to diagnosis and treatment.

*"To administer medicines
to diseases which have already
developed, and to suppress revolts
which have already developed,
is comparable to the behaviour
of those who begin to dig a well
after they have become thirsty,
and of those who begin to cast
weapons after they have already
engaged in battle. Would these
actions not be too late?"*

THE HUANGDI NEIJING

CHAPTER

1

TRADITIONAL CHINESE MEDICINE

Traditional Chinese Medicine (TCM) is based on two foundation stones: qi; and yin and yang. Good health – both physical and emotional – relies on a balance of yin and yang within the body, as an imbalance will cause sickness, disease and sadness. Ancient Chinese doctors were only paid if their patients stayed well, so there has always been an emphasis on avoiding disease in addition to treating it. This chapter shows what qi energy is about, and explains the concept of yin and yang. Here we start to meet the all-important meridians and begin to understand Chinese forms of thinking where health is concerned.

"The part cannot be well unless the whole is well"

PLATO

QI or CHI

Qi or chi refers to the energy that runs through the body.

In Traditional Chinese Medicine, qi is the vital force of life which flows throughout the body through channels, known as meridians.

These meridians connect organs, tissues, veins, nerves, cells, atoms and consciousness.

While the meridians run throughout the body, there are twelve major meridians connecting twelve major organs.

"Where the mind goes, the qi follows. What you focus on becomes your reality."

LORNE BROWN

"We are not meant
to perfect; we are
meant to be whole."

JANE FONDA

YIN and YANG

Yin and yang are the two opposing qualities of qi.

TCM therapists use terms such as night, dark, cold, feminine and negative to describe yin; and day, light, warm, masculine and positive when referring to yang.

Neither yin nor yang is good or bad, and neither is the preferred quality – in TCM, everything needs to be in balance.

An alteration or problem with yin and yang will cause an imbalance in qi, which will result in disease and illness.

The symbol for yin and yang is two fish in a circle – yin is black, and yang is white.

Because yin and yang are complementary rather than antagonistic, the eye of each fish is the opposite colour – illustrating that every yin has a little yang, and every yang has a little yin.

According to Traditional Chinese Medicine, everything can be classified as yin or yang. For example, the spleen, lungs and kidney are yin, while the skin, heart and the liver are yang.

A disease is yin if it is from internal causes and yang if from external sources. As well as within the human body, yin and yang are said to be present in the outer world.

"Yin alone cannot arise;
Yang alone cannot grow.
Yin and yang are divisible
but inseparable."

THE YELLOW EMPEROR

the FIVE ELEMENTS of NATURE

Traditional Chinese Medicine also believes that humans are merely microcosms of the wider universe and are therefore connected to, and subject to, the forces of nature.

There are five elements to the forces of nature, which are: *Earth* (tu), *Fire* (huo), *Water* (shui), *Wood* (mu) and *Metal* (jin).

To remain healthy, we must achieve a balance between our internal organs, through qi and yin and yang, and the external world, the elements of nature.

Each element has corresponding organs and parts of the body, seasons, qualities and even colours and tastes.

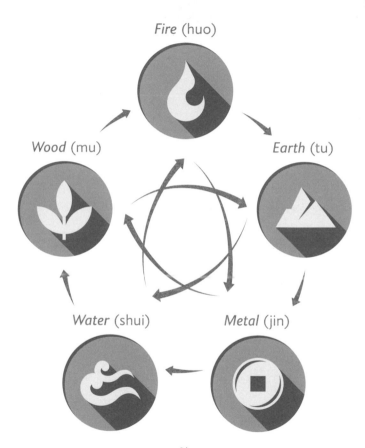

Fire (huo)

Wood (mu)

Earth (tu)

Water (shui)

Metal (jin)

EARTH

The element Earth is associated with the colour
yellow. It symbolizes transformation, creativity
and worry, and its corresponding organs are the
spleen and the stomach. It is also associated with
the mouth, late summer and a sweet taste. Any
imbalance in the spleen or stomach meridians may
result in stomach pain or digestive issues or worry.
At the same time, a balanced Earth element would
promote transformation and creativity.

FIRE

The element Fire is represented by the colour red and is associated with joy, growth, summer and a bitter taste. Its corresponding organs are the mouth, the heart and the small intestine. So, a healthy heart meridian when yin and yang are balanced will lead to joy and happiness.

WATER

The element Water is, perhaps surprisingly,
associated with the colour black.
Less surprising is that it is connected to a salty
taste, the bladder and the kidneys. Water is
also linked to the ear and to feelings of fear
and to winter.

WOOD

The element of Wood is associated with the colour green, and it represents both birth and anger. The eyes, gallbladder and liver are the body parts associated with Wood, as are the season of spring and a sour taste. So, perhaps a woman struggling to conceive has an imbalance of chi in her liver meridian that needs to be dealt with.

METAL

The element of Metal is associated with the colour white, the season of autumn and a pungent taste. It is linked to the lungs, the large intestine and the nose, and the qualities of grief and harvest, or, alternatively, plenty. According to Traditional Chinese Medicine, a person's grief and sadness could be due to a problem with their intestine.

A RANGE of THERAPIES

A TCM practitioner is a very skilled and experienced professional. He or she will be well regarded within Chinese society and consulted whenever there is a worry about health – whether physical or emotional.

The therapist will use smell, hearing, voice vibration, touch, pulse and even a tongue diagnosis to identify imbalance and illness.

Once diagnosed, the healer will use a combination of a range of ancient Chinese therapies to treat the patient.

There are several different therapies available within Traditional Chinese Medicine, including acupuncture, acupressure and moxibustion. All TCM treatments are based on the foundations of qi, yin and yang, and the five elements of nature.

With acupuncture, thin needles are inserted into different points along the meridian lines, and acupressure replaces needles with finger pressure, while moxibustion involves the burning of herbs at these acupuncture points.

These, and other therapies, are all described in Chapter 3 starting on page 42.

CHAPTER

2

the HISTORY of
TRADITIONAL
CHINESE
MEDICINE

As you can imagine, Chinese medicine has a long history, and it probably goes back many millennia further than the written records we have available for study today.

Ancient methods of understanding the body and treating it would have been passed on orally from master to student or father to son. There must also have been many "wise women" who treated women for menstrual problems, childbirth and who had a myriad common household cures for common problems. Later, the situation became more formal, with trained doctors and written texts that could be copied by those who were at a distance from the doctor.

What we do know is that the first written record of Traditional Chinese Medicine is from the third century BC: what has become known as *The Yellow Emperor's Inner Canon*. This was the first book to mention the relationship between yin and yang, the concept of qi, the functions of the human body and the five phases of nature.

By the year 220 AD, the first book on drugs and herbal medicine – *The Treatise on Cold Injuries* – was written by Zhang Zhongjing. This was eventually followed by the most detailed manual on herbal medicine – the *Bencao Gangmu* by Li Shizhen – in the mid-1500s. This listed a total of 1,892 drugs known to Chinese medicine and 11,000 separate prescriptions for ailments.

By the 1800s, however, Western missionaries and doctors began to flock to China, bringing with them their own medical texts and knowledge. This started the slow but steady attempt to move away from ancient medical practices in China.

Diseases such as blackwater fever, cholera, plague, smallpox, scarlet fever, malaria and diphtheria were still clearly a problem in the early 1900s, so a much greater emphasis on public hygiene along with a preference for Western medicine grew. More laws and regulations relating to public health were passed, and Traditional Chinese Medicine became a symbol of old, backward ways.

In 1929 a proposal entitled *A case for the Abolishment of the Old Traditional Chinese*

Medicine to Thoroughly Eliminate Public Health Obstacles was published by Yu Ai and Wang Qizang. This prevented the setting up of new Chinese medicine schools while limiting advertising for the practice of TCM.

However, the complete eradication of TCM proved to be impossible. On 17 March 1929, members of 132 TCM associations met in Shanghai and set up the National Union for Traditional Chinese Medicine – an organization that was designed to champion the cause of TCM and remind people of its benefits.

Traditional Chinese Medicine remained popular among the poor, especially in the countryside, where some 80 per cent of the Chinese population lived at the time. Mao Zedong himself, in the years before the

Cultural Revolution, encouraged the practice of TCM, as he thought it made Chinese communism unique. It also meant that China did not have to rely so much on the West and the Soviet Union for its medicines.

The Cultural Revolution (1966–76) soon changed things. Suddenly traditional culture, philosophical thinking and academia were crushed by the government. Professors, doctors, teachers and the well-educated were targeted, while farmers, labourers and the uneducated gained prominence and prestige. Tens of thousands of Traditional Chinese Medicine practitioners were killed, imprisoned or sent to indoctrination camps in remote parts of the country. A phenomenon known as "barefoot doctors" emerged, whereby uneducated, untrained and ill-equipped labourers from the countryside became the only means of healthcare outside the cities. By 1984 there were thought to be 1.28 million barefoot doctors practising a crude form of Western medicine.

By 1976, however, at the end of the Cultural Revolution, academia, the arts, culture and TCM began to slowly re-emerge, and even now it remains very much a fixture of Chinese society alongside Western medicine. The medical profession has adopted a fusion of the two systems, taking the best from each.

Indeed, within China today, there is a three-tier system: Traditional Chinese Medicine; Western medicine; and an integrated model combining both. This has opened up choice and self-determination for the Chinese people, who now have the best of both worlds available to them.

All this has happened while, at the same time, TCM has gained in popularity in the West.

"Good medicine
tastes better."

CHINESE PROVERB

CHAPTER

3

a description of

ANCIENT CHINESE THERAPIES

This section gives a list of methods of diagnosis and types of treatment using ancient Traditional Chinese Medicine.

Some of these therapies have crossed over into the Western world and become familiar, while others are still strange to us.

"The doctor of the future will give no medicine but will interest his patients in the care of the human frame, in diet and in the cause and prevention of disease."

THOMAS EDISON

ACUPUNCTURE

Acupuncture, one of the oldest theories and practices of Traditional Chinese Medicine, is believed to correct energy imbalances and restore good health. Acupuncture points are found at precise locations along meridian lines across the whole body, and the treatment will enhance the flow of qi and balance yin and yang.

After a consultation with a qualified acupuncture therapist, special needles are inserted into acupuncture points at various places on the body.

These needles are exceptionally fine and only a centimetre or so in length. They may be inserted just underneath the skin or pushed further into muscle and are left in place for up to 30 minutes.

"The World Health Organization has recognized acupuncture as effective in treating mild to moderate depression."

TIM DALY,
AMERICAN ACTOR AND PRODUCER

The acupuncturist will use a range of diagnostic tools to work out what the issue is, and which acupuncture points need to be used.

The inserted needles act to unblock that specific meridian line and thus allow qi to flow correctly.

There should not be any pain during an acupuncture session – perhaps just some tingling or a dull ache where the needles are inserted.

After treatment, in addition to improved symptoms of any pre-existing condition the patient has, he should also enjoy a general feeling of wellbeing and relaxation.

Acupuncture is used for multiple purposes. Specifically, it is thought to help with:

Giving up addictions such as smoking

Post-operative dental pain

Nausea and sickness caused by chemotherapy

Headaches

Migraines

Joint pain

Stroke rehabilitation

Asthma

Carpal tunnel syndrome

Back pain

Menstrual pain

ACUPRESSURE

Acupressure is a massage technique similar to acupuncture, using the same acupuncture points. However, it replaces needles with pressure from fingers, palms, elbows, feet and knuckles.

A fully clothed patient would lie on a massage table for a session that typically lasts between 30 and 60 minutes.

The acupressure points are gradually pressed with a gentle but firm pressure, which lasts from 30 seconds to two minutes at each location.

some common
ACUPRESSURE POINTS
for self-healing

TRIPLE ENERGISER 3 / ZHONG ZHU

This will help treat a headache, shoulder and neck tension, and upper back pain. The pressure point is found beneath the lower knuckles of the hand, between the tendons of the fourth and fifth fingers. Use a thumb or finger from the other hand to apply deep, firm pressure to the point for four to five seconds.

SPLEEN 6 / SAN YIN JIAO

This is for urological, pelvic disorders,
insomnia and menstrual cramps. Locate
the highest point of your ankle then
place four fingers above this, on the
inside of the leg, to find the pressure
point. Apply pressure and massage to
this point for four to five seconds.

Do not do this if you are pregnant.

LIVER 3 / TAI CHONG

This will help lower back pain, stress, high blood pressure, menstrual cramps, insomnia and anxiety. The Tai Chong acupressure point is located on the top of your foot between your big toe and the next two, about two centimetres up the foot.

Pressure should be applied here for four to five seconds.

LARGE INTESTINE 4 / HE GU

This is used for facial, neck and tooth pain, headaches and stress. Have your hand with the thumb and side of the index finger facing towards you. Place your thumb on the index finger to make a triangle or tent shape. The pressure point can be found just under the knuckle of the index finger.

Again, apply firm pressure and massage to this point for four to five seconds.

STOMACH 36 / ZU SAN LI

This is for nausea and sickness, stress and fatigue, and any gastrointestinal issues. Find the pressure point four finger-widths down from the kneecap on the outside of the leg.

If you move your foot up and down, a muscle should appear to "pop out" – this is the spot to apply pressure for four to five seconds.

PERICARDIUM 6 / NEI GUAN

This should relieve nausea, upset stomach, travel sickness, carpal tunnel syndrome and headaches. Turn your palm up and locate the pressure point about three centimetres away from the wrist between the two tendons.

GALLBLADDER 20 / FENG CHI

Pressure and massage at this
acupressure point will help headaches,
migraines, fatigue, low energy and cold
and flu symptoms. Interlace your fingers
and then position your hands on the
back of your head with thumbs
pointing down.

Using your thumbs, you should massage
the area where the neck muscles attach
to the skull, along the ear bone.

GALLBLADDER 21 / JIAN JING

This is used for pain, headaches, shoulder tension and neck stiffness. Pinch your shoulder muscle with your thumb and index finger.

Apply downward pressure and massage for four to five seconds.

Acupressure has a multitude of benefits, including:

- Pain relief – acupressure releases endorphins which help to reduce aches and pains. It is therefore beneficial to sufferers of headaches, arthritis, fibromyalgia and those in chronic pain

- Boosting the immune system and thus increasing resistance to illness

- Detoxing the body and balancing the meridians

- Relieving muscular tension in the back, neck and shoulders

- Promoting healing after surgery or injury

- Releasing emotional blockages to ease emotional pain, stress, trauma and addictions

- Enhancing the tone of facial muscles

- Increasing the blood circulation to the face to decrease wrinkles

It is also possible to have focused acupressure treatment for weight loss, maternity, infertility and even sexual dysfunction.

In addition to seeing a therapist, it is also possible to learn how to self-administer acupressure, which is really useful when suffering from a headache or cold, or if you have a sleep problem.

"*I get a lot of the ideas when I am resting – either when I'm meditating or getting some kind of work done on my back, like acupuncture. That's where I get my best ideas, maybe because I am balancing my body.*"

KATY PERRY,
AMERICAN SINGER

CHINESE ASTROLOGY

In China, Chinese astrology is much more than a fortune-telling tool. It is often used as a therapy, with astrological readings used to detect energy imbalances and ways to rectify them.

According to Chinese astrology, a person's destiny can be determined at birth by the movement of the heavens and plotted onto a chart called "The Four Pillars".

New parents will often pay to have a baby's astrological chart drawn up, and it is still a widespread practice in the markets of China.

CHINESE HERBAL MEDICINE

Chinese Herbal Medicine (CHM) has been a mainstay of Chinese culture since the third century AD.

A Chinese herbalist has the use of more than 300 different herbs to tailor-make a herbal cocktail to help ailments such as depression, anxiety, eczema, gastrointestinal complaints and respiratory problems.

Each prescription will include one or two herbal ingredients targeted at the patient's illness, plus more herbs to suit the patient's yin and yang balance.

The ability to combine the right concoction of herbs and other ingredients is considered an art form in Chinese society.

The balance between the ingredients is thought to be more important than the individual herbs themselves – the sum being more important than the individual parts.

Herbalists will take ingredients from all parts of the plant – roots, leaves, stems, flowers and fruits – plus some ingredients from animals and minerals.

The use of endangered animal parts, such as rhino horns and tiger bones, is controversial now and subject to animal rights protests, so these days, many herbalists avoid those ingredients.

For therapeutic uses, Chinese herbs are consumed either in tablet form or in a decoction, which is a strong tea, simmered for at least an hour.

The herbs used in Chinese Herbal Medicine are categorized according to three criteria:

the four natures

This is the degree of yin and yang within the herb, in terms of cold or hot.

the five tastes

Herbs will have one of five tastes – pungent, sweet, sour, bitter or salty. Each taste shows a use for a different ailment or illness; for example, pungent herbs generate sweat, while sour herbs nourish the liver.

the meridians

Certain herbs are linked with specific meridians, and therefore act on the associated organs.

commonly used
CHINESE HERBS

- **ginger** is a spicy herb which can be used to help digestion and nausea. It can improve blood circulation and is often used to treat coughs caused by colds.

- **salvia** helps repair damaged body tissue following injury. It can help reduce chronic inflammation and infection. It is also suitable for lowering blood pressure, reducing cholesterol and aiding liver function.

- **liquorice** helps digestion and reduces inflammation.

- **ciwujia** is a popular anti-ageing herb which can help with weight loss. It is also used to prevent fatigue.

- **roseroot** has been used to treat cancer, tuberculosis and diabetes, as well as increasing immunity. It is a versatile herb which can also help prevent colds and flu while enhancing physical strength and endurance.

- **astragalus** contains antioxidants which protect against cell damage and may help prevent diseases such as cancer and diabetes while also treating heart disease. It can also be used to strengthen the immune system and prevent colds and flu from developing.

- **reishi** mushrooms are another antioxidant which can protect the immune system against colds and flu. Reishi mushrooms can also reduce blood sugar levels and blood pressure.

- **cannabis** has a long history of being used in Chinese Herbal Medicine. Taken in the form of a juice or a capsule or applied externally as oil, it can help with dry coughs, backache, epilepsy, asthma and general pain relief.

CHINESE
NUMEROLOGY

In traditional Chinese culture, some numbers are considered auspicious, while others are not so favourable.

Usually based on the pronunciation of the number in either Mandarin or Cantonese, different numbers have a different significance to everyday life.

The Chinese will often plan weddings and celebrations on specific dates according to numerology or avoid dates if the number is considered unlucky.

zero is considered a respectable number, as it signifies the beginning of things.

one is neither good nor bad. On the one hand, it can signify a winner; on the other, it can symbolize loneliness or being single. Interestingly, 11 November each year is a special day for single people in China.

two is a good number and is said to represent the phrase "good things come in pairs". It is related to good luck and prosperity.

three is seen as both auspicious *and* inauspicious. It is associated with the three stages of life: birth, marriage and death. However, the pronunciation in Mandarin sounds like *split* or *separate* and can be interpreted as a bad number.

four is a very unlucky number because, in Mandarin, it is spelt the same way as the word *death*. It is such an unlucky number that many Chinese buildings do not have a fourth floor!

five is an important number in Chinese numerology, as it is associated with the five elements – Wood, Fire, Earth, Metal and Water.

six is a lucky number in Chinese numerology, especially for business. It is pronounced like the word for happiness and so is associated with good fortune.

seven is another number that can be both good and bad. On the one hand, it is thought as a good signifier of relationships because it sounds like *arise* or *even*. Still, on the other hand, it also sounds like *to deceive* in Mandarin.

eight is the most auspicious number in Chinese numerology – being associated with joy, happiness and prosperity. A collection of 8s is considered even luckier. The Beijing Olympics in 2008 started on 8 August at eight minutes past eight.

nine is often seen as a good number for anything associated with weddings because it sounds like *long-lasting*.

"He that takes
medicine and neglects
diet wastes the skill
of the physician."

CHINESE PROVERB

CHINESE NUTRITIONAL THERAPY

Ancient Chinese culture recognizes that food affects the body and energy flow and that it has specific therapeutic properties.

In Traditional Chinese Medicine, there is
no distinct difference between food and
medicine.

Within Chinese nutritional therapy,
each food, herb or spice is classified
according to its nature, which may be
hot, cold, warm, cool or neutral.

Depending on its category, the food will
be beneficial to specific organs, parts of
the body, conditions or ailments.

Cinnamon, for example, is warm, pungent and sweet. It is especially useful for digestive problems because these are usually caused by coldness in the stomach according to the practice. Strawberry is cool, and therefore an excellent food to eat if you are suffering from hot flushes.

A Chinese nutritional therapist, after the first consultation, can devise an individualized diet and meal plan. This would be based on the specific diagnosis and individual needs.

It is believed that learning how to nourish your body will help:

Prevent illness

Remove disease

Weight loss

Increase strength

Increase life expectancy

Remove energy blockages

CUPPING

What do Hollywood stars Gwyneth Paltrow and Jennifer Aniston have in common with sportsmen Michael Phelps and Alex Naddour? Well, they have all been photographed with red circular marks on their backs – the tell-tale signs of being advocates of cupping, or myofascial decompression to give it its proper name.

"*Eastern medicine has a different approach than Western medicine – it's more holistic. The root of the problem is addressed, as opposed to a symptom being dealt with, using prescription medication, only to return. I've been helped tremendously by various practices that help the body heal itself.*"

GWYNETH PALTROW,
WRITING ON HER LIFESTYLE WEBSITE GOOP
IN 2009

Traditionally used in Chinese therapy to increase blood circulation and improve qi or energy flow, cupping is now used around the world for a wide range of claimed benefits – especially pain relief and relaxation. Cupping, or *ventosa massage* as it is sometimes called, can also help reduce anxiety, depression and stress.

Physical pain and long-term injuries can have a severe impact on mental health. So, helping to treat the root of any physical symptoms can make a positive contribution towards reducing associated depression and worry.

Cupping was formally discovered in China over 5,000 years ago, with the first documented reference to the practice being found in Egypt in 1550 BC.

It was commonly practised in the Roman and Islamic Empires, and in Central and South Asia. Cupping then became a popular treatment in 18th- and 19th-century Europe.

Such is its importance in Chinese society that cupping is now an established therapeutic practice in hospitals and clinics all over China.

"Acupuncture and cupping, more than half of the ills cured."

A FAMOUS CHINESE SAYING ATTRIBUTED TO
GE HONG (281–341 AD)

So … what is cupping?

A therapist will heat up a glass cup using a flame. As the flame goes out, the cup will be placed on the skin.

As the air inside the cup cools down, a vacuum is created, which makes the blood vessels expand. The cup is left in place for three minutes.

Sometimes a silicone cup is used that is moved from place to place, giving a massage-like feeling at the same time.

There is also a variation known as wet cupping – after the cup is removed, tiny cuts to the skin are made using a scalpel. A second suction draws out a small quantity of blood to remove toxins directly from the body.

After a cupping session, you should relax, drink water and keep the suctioned area out of sunlight. Showering or bathing, drinking alcohol or exercising is not recommended for at least 24 hours.

Because of the toxins being flushed out of the system, the patient might feel nauseous or have a headache or flu-like symptoms, but these will soon pass.

It goes without saying that you should only receive cupping therapy from a qualified professional.

The treatment should not be painful or uncomfortable. Still, it should be avoided by those who are pregnant, have a heart condition, a fever or allergic skin conditions.

Those with autoimmune diseases or problems with the lymphatic system should also avoid cupping.

Cupping therapy might be able to help the physical symptoms of:

- Skin conditions such as acne and eczema
- High blood pressure
- Congestion caused by sinusitis, allergies and asthma
- Varicose veins
- Blood disorders such as haemophilia and anaemia
- Injuries such as torn muscles and tendons, and sporting strains
- Headaches and migraines
- Pain from rheumatic diseases such as fibromyalgia and arthritis

EAR CANDLING

Ear candling is a simple, non-invasive method of removing ear wax or other impurities from the ear canal.

You might think that ear candling involves sticking a candle in your ear and lighting it!

Well, that isn't too far from the truth, although the candle is specially designed for this treatment.

A hollow tube is made from cotton fibres, stiffened with pure beeswax and infused with essential oils. The therapist will light the tube and then place it gently into the ear, remaining with the patient throughout.

During the process, the ear will be coated in the melting beeswax, and when the beeswax is removed, ear wax and other impurities will be drawn out as well.

When the candle has burned down to a certain point, it is removed, and gentle massage is applied to that side of the face. The procedure is then repeated with the other ear.

The main reason to have an ear candling session is to clear out the build-up of wax from the ear canal. This will help the patient to hear more clearly, as sound waves will more easily travel through the eardrum.

The procedure can also clear out other toxins from the ear.

Ear candling can also help with the treatment of tinnitus and ringing in the ear. Pressure from behind the eardrum can be eased with ear candling, and this, in turn, may reduce the symptoms of tinnitus.

Medical advice should be sought before embarking on this treatment, though.

Ear candling can also get rid of bacteria and some viral infections of the ear. This may help with the treatment of earaches, headaches or sinus trouble.

Again, medical advice should first be sought, but ear candling will often complement formal medical treatment. However, you should not use ear candling if you think you have an ear infection.

If after swimming you suffer from
your ears being blocked by water, ear
candling is worth trying.

It might also be helpful for itchy ears
caused by an allergy such as hayfever.

Some fans of ear candling even credit
it with balancing their mental state –
boosting mental clarity and awareness.

There are some possible side effects of ear candling that should be considered.

Minor burns are one possibility, given that you are having a lighted candle placed in your ear. Some redness may also occur temporarily around the ear and side of the face after the procedure.

You must always use a professional therapist to administer ear candling.

GUA SHA

At first glance, the practice of Gua Sha might not seem particularly comfortable, given that it does cause some minor bruising to the skin! It's another ancient Chinese therapy that aims to balance the flow of qi or energy around the body.

The name Gua Sha comes from the Chinese word for *scraping*, and this is a good description of what it is: the scraping of the skin to relieve pain, tension and energy blocks.

Gua Sha can also be used to treat inflammation and help the immune system.

A small hand-held tool, with rounded edges, is used to scrape the skin. This is done after applying oil to the relevant body part, often the back or the legs.

The practice of Gua Sha should not hurt or be uncomfortable, and any bruises that are left after the treatment should disappear within a couple of days.

Gua Sha is not suitable for everyone, though, and it should not be conducted on a person who:

- has deep-vein thrombosis
- bleeds easily
- takes medication to thin their blood
- has an implant such as a pacemaker

MASSAGE

Massage as a form of Traditional Chinese Medicine goes back almost 4,000 years. There are two main types of massage available in Traditional Chinese Medicine: Tui Na and Zhi Ya. Both types subscribe to the TCM theory that disease, illness, injury and imbalance cause a blockage in the meridians, which leads to pain.

Traditional Chinese Medicine massage therapy can:

- Increase energy
- Encourage relaxation
- Speed up recovery of soft tissue injury
- Boost blood circulation
- Break down scar tissue
- Support emotional health
- Reduce bruising
- Relieve chronic pain
- Strengthen the body's resistance to disease
- Improve athletic performance
- Regulate the nervous system

Traditional Chinese Medicine thinks of massage as being communication between the practitioner's qi and the patient's qi. The patient is even encouraged to talk during the treatment, to release pent-up feelings or blocked emotions.

The patient lies down or stays seated during a massage, fully dressed and covered by a cotton sheet. Aromatherapy oils, especially chosen for the ailments the patient displays, may be used on hands, feet and the neck.

TUI NA

massage

Tui Na is a deep-tissue massage, meaning literally "push and grab". It is the most common of the types of massage within Traditional Chinese Medicine, and it is like the massage we are familiar with in the West.

Tui Na involves massage techniques such as kneading, chopping, perpendicular pressure, hammer vibration and the rolling fist method. It can also include pressure applied by the feet of the therapist.

The primary function is to remove tension in the muscles in addition to unblocking the flow of qi. Tui Na massage involves pressure on specific acupuncture points along the meridian system, depending on what the therapist considers in need of treatment. By removing stagnation and encouraging the blood and qi to flow more freely, the body's self-healing process is stimulated.

A Tui Ma massage will involve an intense, continually moving pressure that might be repeated hundreds of times. The therapist will press hard with the ball of the thumb at a specific acupressure point and then rub lightly around the area.

A Tui Ma therapist may spend as much time in one area, one joint or one muscle as a Western therapist would spend in a whole session.

PAEDIATRIC
massage

Paediatric massage is a form of Tui Na massage adapted for the specific needs of children under the age of 12. In Traditional Chinese Medicine, it is thought that children have fewer physical and emotional barriers. Thus, their qi is more accessible and receptive to treatment.

Sesame oil is used as a massage oil to give very gentle pressure along acupuncture points on the body, with the session usually lasting only 15 to 20 minutes.

Paediatric massage can be used to treat:

- Asthma
- Bedwetting
- Nightmares
- Teething
- Colic
- Nausea
- Fever
- Constipation
- Colds

"*The soft and the pliable will defeat the hard and strong.*"

LAO TZU

ZHI YA

massage

Zhi Ya massage involves pinching and pressing the surface of the skin on the feet and the body along acupuncture points in a comparable way to reflexology.

The aim of Zhi Ya is to relieve strain and stress in large muscle groups.

AN MO

massage

An Mo massage is a less common type of treatment that focuses on restoring vitality. Its name means "press" and "stroke", and it can be practised as part of a martial arts programme as well.

An Mo sessions can take as long as two hours, depending on the ease of qi that flows between the therapist and patient.

It is a full-body treatment that has a set pattern of movements and techniques based on a yang routine to break up blockages and a yin routine to soothe and calm the body.

MEDITATION

Meditation is an integral part of
Traditional Chinese Medicine. As
with all ancient Chinese therapies,
meditation helps to clear qi
blockages and balance yin and yang
within the body and mind.

During a meditation session, the patient
can experience immediate relaxation,
a sense of peace and tranquillity and a
lowering of their blood pressure.

When practised regularly, meditation
also has longer-term benefits such
as improving the immune system,
increasing the ability to focus and giving
a general sense of wellbeing.

Meditation is not sleeping, nor is it unconsciousness – it is merely a profound sense of relaxation, stillness and inner focus. The person stays awake and is aware of their surroundings.

A simple way to meditate is to close your eyes and focus on breathing while it flows in and out. You can silently count your inhales and exhales if that helps you focus.

You can also conduct a full-body scan by turning your whole attention to one part of the body at a time; for example, the right big toe. Imagine sending your breath to that area and then move on to the next toe.

Continue until you have scanned your whole body – right and left, front to back, toes to head.

Contrary to widespread belief, you are not expected to empty your mind, because thoughts cannot be consciously stopped.

What you should do when an unwelcome or unwanted thought creeps into your meditation is acknowledge it and let it pass. Don't hold on to it and don't analyse it – just let it go.

Chinese meditation can be used in conjunction with any other form of Traditional Chinese Medicine to give a completely holistic experience.

MOXIBUSTION

Moxibustion is a traditional Chinese therapy which involves burning small cones of dried mugwort (an aromatic plant) on various parts of the body – generally the same points as those used in acupuncture.

In ancient China, it was believed
that burning or heating certain parts
of the body increased circulation and
relieved pain.

The practice was first developed in
northern China and was used to treat
the symptoms of rheumatism.

Originally, moxibustion resulted in the
development of blisters at the "burn"
site, but in modern practice the skin is
simply heated rather than burned.

The mugwort is compressed into a
stick-like shape, not unlike a cigar.
It is lit and then smouldered over a
specific body part about a centimetre
above the skin.

A sudden flooding of warmth along
the site is usually experienced,
showing that the qi or energy has
been unblocked.

It is not uncommon for a moxibustion
treatment to take place alongside
acupuncture.

Moxibustion is recommended for:

Arthritis

Digestive problems

Joint pain

Colds and flu

MUSIC THERAPY

Chinese music therapy is an established part of Traditional Chinese Medicine and has its roots in Taoism.

Within TCM, it is thought that the correct combination of rhythm, timbre and energy within a musical piece balances yin and yang.

The belief is that inner harmony (within the body) can be achieved through outer harmony, and vice versa. Classical Chinese musical instruments include the drum, gong, flute and zither.

"*Harmony between music and man, harmony between heaven and man.*"

CHINESE PROVERB

As with all aspects of Traditional Chinese Medicine, music is closely connected to the five elements, or "five phases" as the elements are sometimes referred to.

According to ancient Chinese thought, each musical note is associated with one of the elements, and each corresponds to the internal organs. Specific imbalances of yin and yang within the body can be improved by listening to certain tones of music.

jiao is the equivalent of the Western musical note "E". It represents the element of Wood and is known as the sound of spring. It promotes the correct functioning of the liver and relieves depression.

zhi or "G" is connected to Fire, and it represents summer. The organ it rules is the heart, and it is said to invigorate blood flow.

gong or "C" is associated with Earth and late summer. It strengthens and nourishes the spleen.

shang or "D" is connected to Metal and autumn, and it protects the lungs.

yiu or "A" is linked to water, winter and the kidneys.

REFLEXOLOGY

Reflexology is a type of massage applying different amounts of pressure to the feet, hands and ears.

In Traditional Chinese Medicine, various body parts correspond with varying points of pressure.

Reflexology applies pressure to these points to unblock qi or energy in the relevant part of the body.

Distinct parts of the toes, the sole,
the heel and other sections of the foot
correspond to different areas in the
body. For example, part of the big toe
is linked to the head, while the heel
corresponds to the lower back.

Reflexologists will massage and apply
pressure to the big toe to relieve a
headache.

The ear represents a multitude of body parts. For example, the opening of the ear canal corresponds to the oesophagus and part of the ear lobe is associated with the neck and jaw.

It is a similar story with the hands; for example, the outside of the wrist represents the ovaries while the top of the index finger connects to the head, the face and the sinuses.

Reflexology may help to:

- Reduce pain
- Reduce stress and anxiety
- Improve sense of wellbeing
- Improve mood
- Boost the immune system
- Help treat colds and flu
- Improve back pain
- Improve digestion
- Ease arthritic pain
- Correct hormone imbalances
- Clear sinus blockages

You should not undergo a reflexology treatment if you are suffering from:

- Open wounds on your hands or feet
- Epilepsy
- A low platelet count
- Circulatory problems in the feet
- Blood clots or thrombosis
- Gout
- Fungal infections
- Foot ulcers

TONGUE DIAGNOSIS

According to Traditional Chinese Medicine, the tongue has a relationship with the human body, and it is connected to the meridians and the internal organs. Therefore, TCM practitioners place significant importance on inspecting the tongue when diagnosing illness.

The appearance of the tongue shows whether a person's yin and yang are balanced and whether they are in harmony or disharmony. A normal, healthy tongue is light red or pinkish in colour with a thin white coating.

A Traditional Chinese Medicine practitioner will study the colour of the tongue, its shape, its general appearance, the state of its coating and how moist or dry it is to diagnose illness and disease. This information will help the therapist decide which Chinese therapy to prescribe for the patient.

According to TCM, the appearance of a "normal" tongue will differ according to several factors:

THE SEASONS

- In summer, the tongue coating may be damper and thicker with a slight yellow colouring

- In autumn, the tongue may be thinner with a drier coating

- In winter, the tongue may be damper

- In spring, the tongue should be "normal"

THE TIME OF DAY

As the day progresses, the body
of the tongue becomes more red
and shiny, and the coating becomes
thinner.

THE AGE OF THE PATIENT

In an older person, the tongue is likely
to be dry with cracks, perhaps due
to a reduction in qi. In contrast, in a
child, the tongue is expected to have
a thicker white coating than it would
for an adult.

THE SIZE OF THE PATIENT

Overweight patients tend to have larger tongues that are damper and lighter in colour. The tongues of thin patients, by contrast, are often thinner and redder in colour.

In Traditional Chinese Medicine, distinct parts of the tongue represent different organs of the body:

- The back of the tongue represents the kidney, the bladder and the intestines

- The middle of the tongue represents the stomach and the spleen

- The liver and the gallbladder are represented by both sides of the tongue

- The tip of the tongue rules the heart

- The lungs are represented by the area directly in from the tip

ZHENGGUSHU

Zhenggushu is better known as "bone-setting", which is an ancient Chinese practice for the treatment of fractures, which is rarely available outside of the country.

For centuries, bone-setting has been a popular remedy for broken bones, due to it costing much less than conventional, Western-type treatment. Despite it becoming less common in China today, there are still some orthopaedic hospitals that offer the therapy.

Bone-setting involves the doctor gently manipulating the fractured bone before briskly pushing the bone back into place. In the past, it was done without pain relief, but these days anaesthesia is used. The limb is then wrapped in bandages, slings and a splint – the slight movement of which helps re-join the bone.

Traditional Chinese Medicine also uses another bone-setting tradition, namely medicated "plasters", using a thick liquid known as Zheng Gu Shui. A mixture of herbs, including ginseng, cinnamon, angelica, gentian, inula, menthol and camphor, are grounded into a powder and boiled in a pot of sesame oil, or sometimes alcohol.

The concoction is heated to a temperature of 300 degrees centigrade and then simmered for 10 hours. Then, the liquid is poured onto a coarse cloth, and this is then applied to the relevant part of the body that needs healing.

Zheng Gu Shui is used to reduce qi and blood stagnation, promote healing and soothe pain.

It is often used for the following conditions:

Backache

Arthritis

Strains

Sprains

Bruises

Plantar fasciitis

CHAPTER

4

EXERCISE and MARTIAL ARTS

Doctors the world over recommend exercise, such as gardening, walking, sports or dancing, because any kind of general activity gets things moving, and it is good for the body in so many ways. However, the Chinese especially recommend Tai Chi and Qigong for physical, mental, emotional and spiritual healing, as you will see in this chapter.

Tai Chi and Qigong are closely related and have their roots in Traditional Chinese Medicine. Both are Chinese martial arts dating from the 13th century.

Thinking of martial arts might conjure up images of kicking, punching, fighting and body contact. However, Tai Chi and Qigong focus on slow, flowing body moves to enhance inner calm and peace and relaxation.

TAI CHI

Tai Chi focuses the mind solely on sedate, contemplative movement which soothes the soul and leads to mental calm and clarity. It was originally taught as a self-defence tool with a difference.

According to ancient Chinese wisdom, meeting brute force with brute force only results in injuries for both sides.

"Tai Chi does not mean oriental wisdom or something exotic. It is the wisdom of your own senses, your own mind and body together as one process."

TIM DALY,
AMERICAN ACTOR AND PRODUCER

Tai Chi students were taught to meet violence and aggression with softness and to follow the motion of the opponent until the force of attack exhausted itself. In other words – meeting yang with yin.

Today in China, Tai Chi classes are held in hospitals, clinics, schools, community centres, parks and other outside spaces.

As a low-impact, gentle exercise, Tai Chi is popular with people of all ages and is particularly suitable to the older person or those who prefer slow-paced movement.

Tai Chi can improve posture, balance and mobility while also stimulating blood flow and building up muscle strength in the legs.

Tai Chi is also suitable for dealing with anxiety, depression and low mood. It can aid better sleep and even promote weight loss. In older adults, Tai Chi can improve cognition skills such as memory and decision-making. It can also reduce the risk of older adults falling and tripping, as they become more aware of their movements.

Tai Chi can help those who live with chronic conditions such as Parkinson's disease, diabetes, chronic obstructive pulmonary disease (COPD), some cancers, arthritis and fibromyalgia.

There are five distinct styles of Tai Chi:

yang focuses on slow, graceful, relaxing movements. It is a good starting point for those new to Tai Chi, with 24 actions, all carried out with a wide stance and bent knees.

wu requires a higher stance and has 24 to 36 movements in a sequence. It is very, very slow and it concentrates on micro-movements.

chen has 20 moves and incorporates both slow and fast movements.

sun is like Chen, but has fewer crouching, kicking and punching moves.

hao is less commonly practised in the West. It has a very concentrated focus on exact positioning during movement and internal core strength.

Whichever style you choose, Tai Chi is a moving meditation, with poses and movement that flow together without pausing between each of them.

It has often been described as looking like a slow, graceful dance.

*"Think of the circular path
of each movement,
in Tai Chi every movement
is in a curve or circle
that has no ending and
no beginning."*

PAUL LAM

QIGONG

Qigong is strongly associated with Tai Chi; indeed, Tai Chi is sometimes described as being a form of Qigong.

The main differences between the two are that Qigong concentrates on the breath, so postures can be carried out while lying or sitting as well as standing.

As we already know, qi means "breath" or "air", and it is considered the life force within Traditional Chinese Medicine.

Gong means "work" or "effort" – so the practice of Qigong is simply "breath work".

Since 1989, Qigong has been a "standard medical technique" within the Chinese healthcare system.

Doctors in China will prescribe a course of Qigong practice for a range of health conditions, such as:

Hypertension
Lower back and leg pain
Insomnia
Chronic fatigue syndrome
Cervical spondylosis
Menopause
Obesity
Tumours and cancers
Myopia
Coronary artery disease
Peptic ulcers
Chronic liver disease
Diabetes

"Qigong is a way of being.
Being soft yet firm.
Qigong is a way of breathing.
Breathing deeply yet calmly.
Qigong is a way of standing.
Alert, yet relaxed."

NIGEL MILLS

There are three distinct types of Qigong:

MEDICAL QIGONG
to heal self and others

MARTIAL QIGONG
for physical prowess

SPIRITUAL QIGONG
for enlightenment

MEDICAL
qigong

This is very much a foundation stone of Traditional Chinese Medicine, and it has similar diagnostic and treatment techniques as other forms of TCM therapies. Individuals can practise Qigong to enhance their own health, banish illness and prevent disease. On the other hand, Qigong can be practised by qualified practitioners who "emit qi" to help others.

Qigong healers deliver healing qi in several ways:

- Through **Qigong massage** – putting hands on the receiver through massage, acupressure or a simple touch

- Through **tool manipulation** – using a pointed object, acupuncture needle, precious metals or stones (such as silver, gold, brass or jade) to manipulate various parts of the body

- Using **item empowerment** – by energizing precious stones and metals, teas, water and herbal concoctions

- Through **qi emission** – by placing hands several inches above the body and emitting qi to dispel negative energies and influences

- By **distance healing** – by focusing on an individual many miles distant, qi energy is delivered through a meditative process similar to prayer

MARTIAL
qigong

This focuses on physical strength, with practitioners being able to break bricks, bend steel wires and place sharp objects in certain vulnerable areas of their bodies.

"*Where there is no movement, there is pain. Where there is movement, there is no pain.*"

TRADITIONAL
CHINESE SAYING

"If you want to be healthy and live to 100, do Qigong."

MEHMET OZ

SPIRITUAL

qigong

This uses mantras, hand positions, sitting meditations and prayers to bring about enlightenment. This form of Qigong is heavily influenced by Buddhism, Taoism and Confucianism. Spiritual Qigong aims to teach self-discipline, self-awareness and harmony with nature.

"Qigong is the art and science of refining and cultivating internal energy."

KEN COHEN

THE PRACTICE OF QIGONG

To begin your Qigong practice, you need to master your breath and concentration:

Sit upright on a chair with your feet on the ground and legs slightly separated. Your torso should be at a right angle to your thighs. Close your eyes and mouth.

Focus on rhythmic breathing with the goal being that the breath rolls in and out smoothly like ocean waves. It should not be rushed.

Stretch your breath by counting your inhales and exhales. Inhale for six counts, hold your breath for two counts and then exhale for six counts.

Repeat this cycle for about 10 minutes before returning to your normal breathing rhythm.

Settle your mind by focusing entirely on your breathing. As thoughts come up, acknowledge them, but then let them float away and return your focus to your breath.

You now need to *relax your body* by performing a body scan. Simply mentally scan through your body, part by part, head to toe, releasing tension as you go.

CHAPTER

5

PHILOSOPHY
and
RELIGION

There are three main philosophies or religions that have influenced Traditional Chinese Medicine for centuries, and these are:

TAOISM (or DAOISM)
BUDDHISM
CONFUCIANISM

TAOISM (or DAOISM)

This ancient Chinese religion is at least 2,500 years old. It believes that words, actions and thoughts can change things in the real world. It considers that opposites rely on each other to exist; for example, light and dark, good and evil, yin and yang.

The focus is on leading a simple and balanced life in harmony with nature, without conflict, as this is the ideal life. Both Tai Chi and Qigong are strongly associated with Taoist thinking.

BUDDHISM

Buddhism came to China in the first two centuries AD. Buddhism believes that mental wellbeing is a pre-condition for physical health, so quietening the mind with focused breath control leads to good health and longevity.

Buddhism shares with Traditional Chinese Medicine a belief in qi as the life force that flows through the body via the meridians. It also believes that maintaining balance is essential to physical and mental health, liberation and, ultimately, enlightenment.

CONFUCIANISM

The Chinese have followed Confucianism for more than two millennia, and it is still very much the foundation of Chinese society, along with its values and norms. Not just a religion, it is an all-encompassing way of thinking and living.

In terms of Traditional Chinese Medicine, Confucianism focuses on the wholeness of the body, so it is an advocate of acupuncture and herbal remedies. It believes in "objective" medicine rather than superstition and myth, and it endows a higher social standing to medical practitioners.

CONCLUSION

It is surprising how many of these ancient Chinese traditions have continued to exist and be used all these millennia since they were first worked out. Some have gone out of fashion in recent years because they use the parts of endangered animals. In contrast, others damaged the patients while healing them. However, the rejected techniques are very few in comparison to what is still around and in use today.

The shamanic medicines of pre-development countries, and even the situation in the developed West up to a couple of hundred years ago, relied upon a good deal of superstition. Some practitioners used astrology, which works, but "decumbiture" astrology is devilishly difficult to do and very easy to get wrong.

Chinese Traditional Medicine may include some Chinese astrology and Feng Shui, but not all of it does. Although there may be a spiritual element in some systems, treatment doesn't include prayers or the belief that praying can cure someone, or that being touched by a monarch can bring about a cure. It doesn't even rely on such things as crystals.

Chinese Traditional Medicine is practical and sensible, and it has been built on centuries of observation and a long tradition of writing, teaching and use. For the most part, the treatment takes time – which is something Western doctors don't have to offer. Besides, there is a belief that eating well while keeping one's weight within sensible limits, taking some exercise, doing something useful with one's life and avoiding too much stress is a good way of staying as healthy as possible.

And what doctor in any tradition, anywhere and at any time, past, present or future, can argue with that?